Judy and Trudy are best friends.
Judy and Trudy have lots of fun.

1

Judy likes to make Trudy smile.
Judy puts on a hat with blue plumes.

Judy looks cute with the blue plumes.
This does not make Trudy smile.

3

Judy gets a long flute.
Judy plays a silly tune.

Judy looks cute with the flute.
This makes Trudy smile a bit.

Judy makes a house with cubes.
Judy uses the house to hide.

Judy looks cute in the cube house.
This makes Trudy smile a bit more.

The cube house falls down.
Judy has a huge smile.
This gives Trudy a huge smile, too!